BAD WEATHER:
MY FLOOD STORY

Written by Dr. Keke

Pictures by D.Jones

ISBN-10: 1979285675
ISBN-13: 978-1979285674

*Dedicated to all the kids who open their world to us,
all the adults who could never fully be kids,
and all the people who work to help them.*

Dear Caregiver or Parent,

Congratulations on taking a step towards aiding a child in processing emotions and events which impact their life. Adults process information in different ways from children, and books such as this offer an opportunity for children to feel safe.

Bring your crayons and pencils this way… 

WHAT IS WEATHER? IT'S RAIN, SHINE, CLOUDS, AND SNOW. THESE ARE THE TYPES OF WEATHER I KNOW.

______________ IS MY FAVORITE WEATHER.
IT MAKES ME FEEL____________

SOME DAYS THE WEATHER IS BAD! WHEN
IT GETS LIKE THIS I FEEL ______________.

A STORM CAME AND WITH IT THE RAIN. THE RAIN TURNED TO PUDDLES, THE PUDDLES TO RIVERS. FASTER IT CAME! QUICKER AND QUICKER!

RESCUE
21
RSCUE
21
21

__________ SAID WE HAD TO LEAVE. WE PACKED UP SOME OF OUR THINGS.

AWAY WE WENT AND I FELT _______________.

WHAT ABOUT ALL THE STUFF I HAD?

______________ EXPLAINED THE WEATHER WAS BAD, SO PERHAPS WE COULD NOT GO BACK.

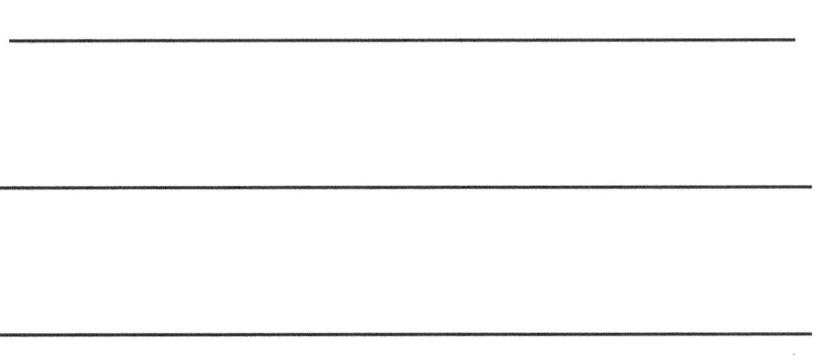

SOME THINGS I HAD, I WILL MISS.
I THOUGHT ABOUT IT. I MADE A LIST:

____

____

____

_________________________ SAYS WE WILL
FIND A NEW HOME. I'LL SHOW IT TO
YOU. I'LL DRAW IT BELOW.

WHEN I FEEL UPSET ABOUT THE WEATHER, WHO CAN I TURN TO, TO HELP ME FEEL BETTER?

____

____

____

I CAN ALSO TAKE A BREATH. BREATHING EXERCISES CAN HELP ME REST. See page 19.

THUNDER, LIGHTNING, RAIN THAT FALLS,
BAD WEATHER IS JUST WEATHER IS ALL.

CONGRATULATIONS! YOU DID IT!

The pages which follow are meant to be supplementary and supportive to this book.

Caregiver Book Guide Tips- *This section contains things to consider before using the book.*

Probing Questions- *These questions are meant to expand upon the content in subsequent readings.*

Praise and Encouragement Suggestions- *While these suggestions may come easy to some, others without much experience working with children may desire some starters.*

Reading Accomplishment Chart- *Children with more behaviors related to the book topic should read this book with the caregiver more frequently initially, with reading "maintenance" as needed. The chart allows you to track each reading.*

Breath Exercise Suggestion/Tracker- *The breath exercise in a simple exercise to assist with stress reduction in people. Practice it with your child to provide them with a coping tool during storms.*

Emotions Chart- *For emotion identification, you may want to detach the chart for children having trouble identifying their feelings.*

These are simply suggestions based on my experiences, training, and interaction with children. However, you know your child best and may need to alter elements of this book. That's okay! The book is meant to spark engagement and processing of emotions for the child.

<u>Caregiver Book Guide Tips</u>

✓ If a child is unable to sit through the entire book, do not force them. It is recommended to set a timer for the amount of time they are able to tolerate, or alternatively, complete one page a day (or sitting).

✓ Allow the child to express the emotion on their own if possible, do not choose for them. For some children, this may take some time (the chart of emotions may help).

✓ If you do not agree with the child's emotion, validate their choice. Do not change their choice, as this may make them feel shame or bad.

✓ If a child is unable to speak, you may use the chart of emotions from the book and allow them to point to feelings.

✓ Some children need more help figuring out the activities or options of what to do once they have identified a feeling. Give them time to think, but also feel free to provide options.

✓ If a child is unable to write, you may write for them in pencil lightly. If they are able to write in the future, this provides an opportunity for them to do so.

✓ Ask the child to read the book back to you (even if they do not know how to read), to see their interpretation of the book and your time together.

✓ Allow or encourage more drawing in the free spaces in the book.

✓ Read more than once the first week of use.

<u>**Caregiver Probing Question Suggestions**</u>

- Can you tell me more about your bad weather story?
- What did you take with you?
- Where did you go after the storm?
- What do you think about storms?
- What do you miss about your old house?
- What do you enjoy doing with your family?
- What was your favorite picture to color/draw in the book?
- What do you like/would you like to see in your new home?
- How does _________ feel about storms?
- Have you gone back to your old house? How did it feel?
- How does your breathing exercise make you feel?

<u>**Caregiver Praise and Encouragement Suggestions**</u>

- You are doing a great job in your coloring.
- Sounds like you were very helpful/brave, during the storm.
- You are doing a great job completing this page.
- I'm so proud of you for doing this with me.
- I like how you are turning the pages nicely.
- That sounds very: scary, sad, etc
- Wow, have many things you miss from your old home, that sounds tough!
- What do you enjoy doing for fun?
- Do you think you could read this to your family today?
- Let's practice your breathing exercise, can you show me how?

- Your Suggestions:

READING ACCOMPLISHMENT CHART

Date	Name	Pages Read/Completed

BREATH EXERCISE SUGGESTION/TRACKER

Breath exercises can help people relax, remove stress, and calm themselves. Practicing will strengthen your ability to call on this exercise as a coping tool.

- o Inhale quickly two times through the nose, like a sniff. **Sniff, Sniff**
- o Exhale out the nose once, one long. **MMMMMMMMmmmmmmm**
- o Inhale quickly three times through the nose, like a sniff. **Sniff, Sniff, Sniff**
- o Exhale out the nose once, one long. **MMMMMMMMmmmmmmm**

Repeat several times until you are calm ☺

Date	Name	Minutes Completed

Stay tuned for more books in our "Tough Topics" series, and be on the lookout for our sister series, "Simply Feelings".

Contact us:drkekebooks@gmail.com

EMOTIONS CHART

RESCUE
21
RESCUE
21
21